# Unfolding Truth Ministry

## Memoirs of Truth
## Messages to Glean From

**Minister Shelia Griggs-Parker**

BK Royston Publishing
P. O. Box 4321
Jeffersonville, IN 47131
502-802-5385
http://www.bkroystonpublishing.com
bkroystonpublishing@gmail.com

© Copyright – 2023

All Rights Reserved. No part of this book may be reproduced, stored in a retrieval system, or transmitted by any means without the written permission of the author.

Cover Design: Elite Book Cover

ISBN-13: 978-1-955063-84-5

King James Version (KJV) – Public Domain
New International Version (NIV) - Holy Bible, New International Version®, NIV® Copyright ©1973, 1978, 1984, 2011 by Biblica, Inc.® Used by permission. All rights reserved worldwide.

Printed in the United States of America

# Dedication

In Loving memory of my mother Missionary Ovela Coe, who made my existence possible by choosing to bear me. My mother led me to Christ and was one of my greatest cheerleaders when I walked down the aisle to give my life to Christ. Without her continued prayers, I do not know where I would be. Missionary Coe was the Treasurer and Prayer Warrior for Unfolding Truth Ministry and she did both ministries with her whole heart until she went home to be with our Lord and Saviour on March 30, 2019. My mother's legacy of helping hurting women will continue to live on in me through Unfolding and the Mission work God puts our hands to until God says, "It is finished."

First Lady, Saundra Rose-Minor, was a member of Unfolding Truth Ministry as my assistant for a few years; she assisted in promoting Unfolding events, making the fliers, she assisted wherever her help was needed. Although Saundra left the Ministry due to marrying a pastor and her duties now overshadowed her duties with Unfolding, her greatest contribution to Unfolding was her insisting that I meet the present Assistant Director, Andrea C. Cody, and insisting to Andrea that she meet me. I can truly say God used Saundra in my life in a great way. Andrea has truly been a Godsend. Saundra Rose-Minor went home to be with our Lord and Saviour in 2002.

Pastor Daniel Isaiah Parker, my pastor and my beloved husband, who preceded me in death on December 12, 2020. He didn't have the opportunity to see this book completed on this side of Heaven. My husband was the master cheerleader of whatever God put my hand to. He was patient, kind, understanding and motivating when it came to Unfolding Truth Ministry. His inspiration will never be replaced and his love for me can never be compared; for he loved me unconditionally from beginning to end. His representation of Christ in my life gives me the motivation and the fight to continue this race. I'm so glad that the race is not given to the swift nor to the strong, but to those who endure until the end.

Thank you,
Shelia

# Acknowledgments

I would like to thank my sister, Barthelma, who shared several years ago the following, "I was on my knees reading the flier, the Holy Spirit said these messages would be a book." Then our God sealed it one day when I asked a question about prospering. When I closed my eyes, He gave me "Memoirs of Truth Messages to Glean from." That very moment, God told me to compose the messages He had given for the themes for the conferences and retreats into a book. In obedience, I have completed this memoir.

I would like to thank each member of Unfolding Truth Ministry, for lending your gifts and talents relentlessly. Without your faithfulness to God first, then to this Ministry, know, without you, there would be no me. Missionary Ovela Coe (Mother), Barthelma Adams (Sister), Evangelist, Luvenia Slaughter, all who have been with this Ministry from inception. Minister Adrianne Carter, 20 years, Camille Springfield, Sherita Hollimon (Praise Team), and Assistant Director, Sister Andrea C. Cody, 26 years, who has been everything and everyone I have needed her to be. Andrea once shared with me that God told her, "Help Shelia." She has done just that excellently. My best friend and confidant.

I would like to thank God, my Lord and Savior, for so great a salvation, for giving His Son to die on the cross for my sins, that through my belief, repentance, confession, and acceptance of His redemptive blood, I have eternal life.

I would like to thank my husband, friend, and pastor, Daniel Isaiah Parker, our church family, True Vine House of Deliverance and all five of my children, Ebony, William, Daniel Jr., Shaterra and Ezekiel, for allowing me to live the dream that God gave me with little to no complaints for all the time I have put into this Ministry and the call on my life and being supportive of the call.

# Table of Contents

| | |
|---|---|
| Dedication | iii |
| Acknowledgements | vii |
| Struggle Driven Life | 1 |
| Find Peace With Your Portion | 5 |
| The Master Gardener | 9 |
| Stop Surface Cleaning; Clean the Whole House | 13 |
| Eve or Esther Which One Are You? | 17 |
| "You Again" | 21 |
| A Worship that Breaks Every Chain | 25 |
| Ready Aim Fire | 29 |
| You Will Bloom in Your Season | 31 |

| | |
|---|---|
| Application No Applicator | 35 |
| Roots No Leaves | 39 |
| Rebuked Distractions | 45 |
| Bubble Bath or Pure Water | 49 |
| Possess It or Lose it | 53 |
| Changing Familiar Approaches and Practices | 55 |
| The Prerequisites for Restoration Repentance, Forgiveness and Acceptance | 59 |
| Scarred for Life | 63 |
| Kept for Purpose | 67 |
| Fulfilled Deficiency | 71 |
| Cut Off, Pruned or Die | 73 |
| A Partial Connection | 77 |
| Keep Plugged In; So we Won't or Continue to Lose Your Valuable Jewels | 81 |
| One Way to Be Healed; Take the Pain | 85 |

| | |
|---|---|
| The Misfit | 89 |
| "70 years God Bore Noah's Embarrassment" | 93 |
| Possess It or Lose It - Poem | 97 |
| The Beauty of A Rose - Poem | 99 |
| What Do You Do? - Poem | 101 |
| About the Author | 105 |

# Struggle Driven Life

Therefore, since we have been justified through faith, we[a] have peace with God through our Lord Jesus Christ, 2 through whom we have gained access by faith into this grace in which we now stand. And we[b] boast in the hope of the glory of God. 3 Not only so, but we[c] also glory in our sufferings, because we know that suffering produces perseverance; 4 perseverance, character; and character, hope. 5 And hope does not put us to shame, because God's love has been poured out into our hearts through the Holy Spirit, who has been given to us. Romans 5:1-5

One day while taking my daily walk for exercise this past summer, I began to talk to the Lord, as usual during those walks. I started thinking about my life and all I've been through, and I asked God at that time of feeling overwhelmed, tired, and questioning my purpose etcetera, why have I struggled so much? I can't just get things and do things like everybody else. I'm always struggling! Well, I was stopped in my tracks again, while complaining, questioning and fretting about my life, that my life has been struggle driven. Yes, I know we've read the book, or at least heard of the book or cliché, "The Purpose Driven Life", but the Holy Spirit said, "The Struggle Driven Life", and at that moment, the Holy Spirit also brought to my remembrance our scripture Romans 5 and said, "It has been through your struggles that you have been drawn closer to God. It has been through your struggles that you have and are learning patience. It has been through your struggles that your faith has increased, and it has been through your struggles that you have hope, and because of this hope, you're not ashamed. This has all been allowed for my glory and you have been carried through these struggles by my grace, that your life may be a representation of God's perseverance, God's love, and God's character.

While penning this flier, I was also reminded of a story my pastor shared with us. A father and son lived on a farm; the little boy used to watch the chickens hatch their **eggs.** He noticed that when the **eggs** were about to hatch, they would move around a lot before the chicks cracked through the **eggs.** One day while waiting for the egg to hatch, he decided to help the baby chick by cracking the egg open. The chick came out and walked around for a little while, but then it died. The boy asked his father with tears in his eyes why he died. The father told him, "Son, it needed the struggle to live. It is in our struggles that we gain strength to live."

The NIV commentary stated, "Suffering produces good results in the believer's life." I could do nothing but laugh and begin to praise God, knowing that every struggle in my life will work together for my good.

Perhaps you have felt your life has been full of suffering and struggles; **well, this one's for you!** Come out and hear a few women share about their "Struggle Driven Life". Let's glean from the Word of God, their experiences, their hope and their victory and what it has produced in their lives. Just know our "Struggle Driven Life", will produce in us our "Purpose Driven Life" for the glory of God.

# Prayerful Reflection

# Find Peace With Your Portion

6 But godliness with contentment is great gain. 7 For we brought nothing into this world, and it is certain we can carry nothing out. 8 And having food and raiment let us be therewith content. 9 But they that will be rich fall into temptation and a snare, and into many foolish and hurtful lusts, which drown men in destruction and perdition. 10 For the love of money is the root of all evil: which while some coveted after, they have erred from the faith, and pierced themselves through with many sorrows. 11 But thou, O man of God, flee these things; and follow after righteousness, godliness, faith, love, patience, meekness. 12 Fight the good fight of faith, lay hold on eternal life, whereunto thou art also called, and hast professed a good profession before many witnesses. 13 I give thee charge in the sight of God, who quickeneth all things, and before Christ Jesus, who before Pontius Pilate witnessed a good confession; 14 That thou keep this commandment without spot, unrebukable, until the appearing of our Lord Jesus Christ: 15 Which in his times he shall shew, who is the blessed and only Potentate, the King of kings, and Lord of lords; 16 Who only hath immortality, dwelling in the light which no man can approach unto; whom no man hath seen, nor can see: to whom be honour and power everlasting. Amen. 17 Charge them that are rich in this world, that they be not highminded, nor trust in uncertain riches, but in the living God, who giveth us richly all things to enjoy; 18 That they do good, that they be rich in good works, ready to distribute, willing to communicate; 19 Laying up in store for themselves a good foundation against the time to come, that they may lay hold on eternal life. 1 Timothy 6: 6-19

To reiterate to some and teach others and yet give confirmation to Timothy's teaching in these profound scriptures that the world looks for their peace in financial and material gain. However, Christians are supposed to find their peace in living a Godly life, which should give them contentment. The Word says when people are drawn away with their own lust and desire, they can find themselves in a trap and a snare which can cause much unnecessary grief. "But Godliness with contentment is great gain, for we brought nothing into this world and we can take nothing out of it."

While driving down a street off Union Avenue in Cleveland, Ohio, I saw an elderly man tending his garden. The homes around him were not to be envied; however, his little home was well-kept and he looked so peaceful. As I continued driving, I said to the Lord, "He looks so peaceful."

The Holy Spirit then said to me, "You need to find peace with your portion."
After that encounter, I was so convicted and then convinced that God wanted Unfolding to share with others the truth that Godliness with contentment will grant you peace.

# Prayerful Reflection

# Prayerful Reflection

# The Master Gardener

I am the true vine, and my Father is the husbandman. 2 Every branch in me that beareth not fruit he taketh away: and every branch that beareth fruit, he purgeth it, that it may bring forth more fruit. 3 Now ye are clean through the word which I have spoken unto you. 4 Abide in me, and I in you. As the branch cannot bear fruit of itself, except it abide in the vine; no more can ye, except ye abide in me.
John 15:1-4 (KJV)

To introduce "The Master Gardener" to those who do not know Him. To share the dangers of being fruitless and to expound on the pruning process necessary to produce more fruit. The key for a successful garden is to abide in the vine.

Unfolding Truth Ministry invites you to be introduced to the True Vine and the Gardener as well as to share with believers the dangers of not producing fruit. In your garden of life, are you using the tools necessary to produce fruit? Is it visible that your weeds have choked out your seeds? If you feel this is your garden, then you must be introduced to "The Master Gardener."

In a garden, you must plant your seeds in good soil. The garden goes through many stages before it brings forth any fruit. For continuous fruit, a thorough pruning must take place.

Do you have the tools necessary and are not using them? Perhaps, you need to hear the danger of a fruitless garden. A branch cannot bear fruit of itself, except it abides in the True Vine.

# Prayerful Reflection

# Prayerful Reflection

# Stop Surface Cleaning; Clean the Whole House

**SCRIPTURE:** Matthew 12:43-45, 13: 3-9 (Parable of the Sower) Matthew 13-18-23 (Meaning of Parable)

One evening while soaking for a bath and contemplating how I needed to clean my house, due to me entertaining myself for a meeting the next day, I began to say within myself, "I will clean the downstairs and the bathroom and just close the doors to the other rooms and clean them later." A still, small voice spoke to me at that moment and said, "Stop surface cleaning; clean the whole house." Immediately, that took me to my spiritual house. If we want to keep our temple holy and clean, we must stop hiding our dirt (sins), secrets (sins) behind our church faces and clichés (which represent surface cleaning). We must open those doors wide and expose the dirt and secrets (sins), so that every room in our spiritual house can be cleaned.

In order for us to be delivered from whatever dirt and secret (sins) that we are ensnared with, we must first make sure that we do not have (as taken from the NIV commentary portion of the scripture). "Self-reformation (perpetrating), without spiritual conversion, (Being Born Again), which can lead to serious ramifications." This is mentioned in Matthew 12: 43-45.

Therefore, there are four responses to the Word of God when we hear it: No response, Emotional response, (surface cleaning), Worldly response, (closing the doors in our house, (sin), and Fruitful response, which produces a crop—a hundred sixty or thirty times what was sown. "He who has ears, let him hear."

# Prayerful Reflection

# Prayerful Reflection

# Eve or Esther Which One Are You?

**SCRIPTURE:** GENESIS 3: 1-6 & ESTHER 4: 13-16

One morning while preparing for work, I began to think about my youngest son Ezekiel. He had gone to Homecoming that weekend and the girl he took really appeared to like my son. However, I began to think about when I was Ezekiel's age, which is sixteen, and reflected on how I was at that age. I became interested in a young man. Even though he was nice and my mother liked him, it was not the will of God that he and I become intimate, no matter how innocent it appeared. We stayed together for a very long time and two beautiful children were born from the relationship. Nevertheless, God has ordained intercourse in marriage only.

I got angry when I thought about how the enemy wants the children of God to continue to compromise the truth and settle. I thought, *not on my watch*, can the enemy have my son. We need, as parents, to watch as well as pray. When our children have company, we need to be right there. We need to monitor our sons and daughters at all times, and we need to stop accepting "This is a new generation, everybody's doing it." We, as women and young ladies, set the standard for our men. Are we Eve or Esther?

In a time when sex, sexual immorality, and "if it feels good just do it" is promoted all around us, we need to say, "Not on my watch." We, as women, need to learn how to say no to sex before marriage and call it what God says it is: fornication. We need to stop breaking up homes in the name of love and call it what God says it is: adultery. We need to stop promoting same sex relationships and call it what God calls it: Unnatural affections, perversion, and it is an abomination to Him. Therefore, it is true by God's standard, it's truth for me. When we do not take a stand and speak truth, we compromise and become spiritual chameleons. We have just allowed the enemy to use us, just as Eve did, and killed a nation because she was disobedient.

However, when we live the truth first, then speak the truth and stand up and tell others the truth, even when it's not popular, when we can be in danger, not just of our life but of losing people out of our life, and take a stand because it's right, it can save a nation, just as Esther did. The question remains, are you Eve or are you Esther? Come out and hear a few women share about their Eve and Esther experiences and how Jesus came that we might have life and have it more abundantly. Won't you grace us with your presence?

# Prayerful Reflection

# You Again

**SCRIPTURE: Hebrews: 12: 1-2 Galatians: 5: 16-26**

One Saturday morning while preparing breakfast, something happened and the very thing I had been praying about, God helping me with unforgiveness and resentment, came back up again. Earlier that same week, I had been looking for a movie. I had seen it numerous times before, but there was urgency for me to find that movie. I didn't find it until that Saturday and it was a hand grab away in the place I'd looked for it earlier that week. The name of that movie is **"You Again"**. Once I began looking at the movie, I understood why God wanted me to watch it and the message behind the movie as well. Basically, it's about generational unforgiveness, which leads to fear, resentment, coveting, low-self-esteem, competition, revenge, deception, jealousy, and anger, and how sometimes we think these things are gone, but situations, people, places and things will confirm that those feelings and emotions are still there. If gone unacknowledged and put on the back burner of our minds, these sins can and will destroy relationships, families, jobs, marriage, friendships, ministry and, ultimately, our witness for Christ. They will keep us drinking and drugging, sad, lonely, angry, bitter, rebellious, revengeful and unable to be the woman of God that He has called us to be. Whatever, your **"You Again"** is to let us come together and get to the root of why we feel the way we do and learn from the Word of God what measures we need to take in order for us to begin the process of healing and changing our lives. We cannot change people, and even some circumstances and some decisions made are irreversible, but we can change. We no longer have to be victims. We can be survivors. The Word of God says, "If you walk in the Spirit, you won't fulfill the lust of the flesh." If you have any question if you're walking in your flesh, let the Scripture help you, for the works of the flesh are manifest, which are, "Fornication, impurity, licentiousness, (absence from restraint), idolatry,( whatever you worship), sorcery, enmities, strife, jealousy, anger, quarrels, dissensions, (usually a disagreement which is violent), factions, (self-seeking), envy, drunkenness, carousing and things like these."

But in contrast, the fruit of the Spirit is, "Love, joy, peace, patience, kindness, generosity, faithfulness, gentleness, and self-control."

# Prayerful Reflection

# A Worship that Breaks Every Chain

SCRIPTURE: ACTS: 16:16-30

This theme came from an experience I had while visiting someone in the hospital. When my daughter and I arrived, there were others present in the room.

There was a man there who was running an instrument across the sick person's body as well as others who were chanting words of praise entangled with speaking of energy and power that came from other gods. After this lady continued to try to mix a lie with truth, I said abruptly, "Let's pray." Immediately, this stopped the false worship.

Taking hands with all those in the room, I began to lift up the only name given among men whereby we can be saved, healed, delivered and brought out—the name of Jesus. Immediately after this happened, the Holy Spirit brought a passage of scripture to my mind; I knew it was in Acts but did not know exactly where it was. However, I was led to look this up on the computer and it was found in Acts 16. When I began to read, after the revelation about this woman was being used by Satan while she was speaking out words about Paul that appeared to be exaltation, but Paul discerned this was not of God and became irritated, because he knew it was not of God, and shut Satan up and down.

Upon this happening, God had me continue to read, and it goes into Paul being arrested and thrown in jail really for nothing, but what the Holy Spirit revealed is that this was directly after he shut the enemies' month and money down. That when we take a stand for Christ and shut the devil up, down or reveal his untruths which may result in his loss of someone, something, or somewhere, to render it powerless. We as children of the Most-High God can expect to be attacked by the enemy.

Paul was imprisoned wrongfully; however, he didn't put up a fight at that time. He freely went into the jail cell, but the one thing they did not count on when they locked him up was that they could not lock out his worship. Paul began to give God high praise and started sing songs of praise, and due to his worship being so pure and profound, his worship reached Heaven and his chains were loosed and he was released to give God glory; even in his imprisonment, he worshiped God, and due to that, others were saved and Satan had to let him go.

"A worship that breaks every chain:• What kind of worship are we offering up to our God; are we worshiping the King of Kings and the Lords of Lords in the midst of our trials, tribulations, disappointments, tragedies, losses, and or embarrassments? Or are we allowing our situations to keep us from worshiping God, therefore remaining bound to the chains? Know that there is a worship that breaks every chain in the midst of all situations and there is a worship that will break every bondage (chain).

# Prayerful Reflection

# Ready Aim Fire

I Samuel 17:32-51

To enlighten some and remind others that we all either had or have or will have a giant in our life. This giant can threaten our health, finances, peace, joy, children, spouse and even our lives. But God! God has equipped the born again believer with what's needed to destroy our giant, and sever it at the root. If we don't have God, unfortunately, we don't have the equipment. David was a boy who knew his God. Although he was small in stature, he possessed the faith of a giant and defeated his enemy. We, too, can possess this level of faith. However, only we can know when we're ready to allow God to take us through the necessary steps to obtain this kind of faith. Are you ready? If so, let's take aim with our weapon, the rock, Jesus Christ. Fire this rock at the target, knock it down, cut the head off and worship God.

Take courage and stand against the giants in your life and defeat them.

# Prayerful Reflection

# You Will Bloom in Your Season

**SCRIPTURE:** GALATIANS: 6:9

While driving down East 79th Street, which has historical housing, I was at a light and began to look at the houses and think to myself, *I bet these were beautiful huge homes at one time.* Two of the houses were condemned and the one I was looking at appeared to be on its way to be condemned, but, there was a **Hydrangea Plant** that had beautiful flowers on it; these are one of my favorite flowers.

What the Holy Spirit spoke to me is that no matter how raggedy, torn up, torn down, broken down our house may be, our spiritual house, financial house, mental house, emotional house and/or physical house may be, when we're rooted in Jesus, - **You Will Bloom in Your Season!'**

In spite of the storms, in spite of the rain, in spite of what it feels like or looks like, as long as the flower or tree is not uprooted, it will bloom. Just as the tulips bloom in the spring, the rose bush blooms in the summer, these annual plants and trees bloom in their season, no matter what!

We have all experienced or will experience one or all of the above seasons in our lifetime; we all have a season to bloom as well. However, the scripture teaches us: "Let us not **grow weary** In well **doing,** for you shall reap in due season if you faint not." Walt on the Lord and be of good courage, and He shall strengthen your heart." "'But, those that wait on the Lord shall renew their strength: "They shall mount up with wings like eagles, they shall run and not be weary and they shall walk and not faint." There is a waiting period involved in order for us to come into our full bloom, but just remember thus saith the Lord: -You will Bloom in Your **Season.**

# Prayerful Reflection

# Prayerful Reflection

# Application No Applicator

James 2:14-26

To remind some and teach others what God is requiring from us as women who say we have faith. Let us reflect on the following: While putting on make-up one morning preparing to go to work, I applied my foundation and went on to apply my eye-shadow. I discovered I had the (application) eye shadow, but I didn't have the brush (applicator); without having them both, one was useless without the other. When walking out of the bathroom, the Holy Spirit inspired me to share this reminder and revelation with us, "Faith without works Is dead." The footnotes from James 2:14 states: "Unproductive faith cannot **save** because it is not genuine faith. Faith and works are like a two-part coupon ticket into Heaven; the coupon of works is not good for passage, and the coupon without faith is not valid if detached from works."

Ladies, God is calling for more from us, women who are willing to produce works and good deeds so we can help His hurting women and children; however, this will require obedience, dedication, sacrifice, passion, and action. How many times has God told us to help and we didn't, or wouldn't meet the needs of our brothers and sisters, and we could have?

"In the same way, faith by itself if not accompanied by action is dead." Are we equipped with the application (Faith) but no applicator (Works); will we be found lacking when Jesus calls us home or when He returns?

# Prayerful Reflection

# Prayerful Reflection

# Roots No Leaves

### Matthew 13:1-9 & 18-23

That same day Jesus went out of the house and sat by the lake. ² Such large crowds gathered around him that he got into a boat and sat in it, while all the people stood on the shore. ³ Then he told them many things in parables, saying: "A farmer went out to sow his seed. ⁴ As he was scattering the seed, some fell along the path, and the birds came and ate it up. ⁵ Some fell on rocky places, where it did not have much soil. It sprang up quickly, because the soil was shallow. ⁶ But when the sun came up, the plants were scorched, and they withered because they had no root. ⁷ Other seed fell among thorns, which grew up and choked the plants. ⁸ Still other seed fell on good soil, where it produced a crop—a hundred, sixty or thirty times what was sown. ⁹ Whoever has ears, let them hear."

¹⁸ "Listen then to what the parable of the sower means: ¹⁹ When anyone hears the message about the kingdom and does not understand it, the evil one comes and snatches away what was sown in their heart. This is the seed sown along the path. ²⁰ The seed falling on rocky ground refers to someone who hears the word and at once receives it with joy. ²¹ But since they have no root, they last only a short time. When trouble or persecution comes because of the word, they quickly fall away. ²² The seed falling among the thorns refers to someone who hears the word, but the worries of this life and the deceitfulness of wealth choke the word, making it unfruitful. ²³ But the seed falling on good soil refers to someone who hears the word and understands it. This is the one who produces a crop, yielding a hundred, sixty or thirty times what was sown."

One day while at work, I went to the window to water my plant and noticed that I saw roots in the grass vase but no leaves. I was going to throw it away, but the Holy Spirit said in a small, still voice, "Don't throw it away, give it another opportunity before destroying it." I then thought about myself and my walk in the Lord. Does it only appear that I'm rooted in the Word of God and living it based on the knowledge that I'm sought after through prayer, studying the Word, and my spiritual experiences in life? If I am rooted, what has changed? Where are the leaves, (fruit)? I suggest you ask yourself this question.

The scripture stated that Jesus spoke many things in parables to his disciples and the people that surrounded him, saying, "Behold the sower went out to sow, and as he sowed some seeds beside the road, and the birds (sin) came and ate them up (no response). I don't really understand the word because they are not saved. Other seeds fell on the rocky places where they did not have much soil and immediately sprang up because they had depth of soil. When the sun had risen, (trouble, trials, test) they were scorched. Because they had no root, they withered away (emotional response receives the Word with joy, but it only lasts a short time, no relationship with God).

Other seeds fell among thorns, and the thorns came up and choked them out (the worries of this life and the deceitfulness of wealth chokes it, yielding unfruitful.) In addition, other seeds fell on the good soil and yielded a crop, some of hundredfold, some sixty and some thirty (fruitful response.) "He that has an ear, let him hear."

However, the blessing is that the Holy Spirit reminded me of all of the chances I have been given to apply the Word to my life and that I continue to receive chances. Nevertheless, as I allowed this plant another chance to produce, I'm expecting something different to happen; if it doesn't produce after I feed it, weed it and fertilize it, I'm left with no choice but to get rid of it before it kills the other roots in the same vase. The word declares, "I will destroy the flesh to save the soul."

Whereas we are more important in the eyesight of God than a plant, remember, God speaks to his own in parables and metaphors, using the natural events to give us a spiritual revelation. Our Father is giving us another opportunity to see where we are in the parable of the sower and make the necessary adjustments before it is too late. God loves us so much that he is long-suffering, not willing that any should perish but that all might come to repentance.

# Prayerful Reflection

# Prayerful Reflection

# Rebuked Distractions

**John 21:21-23**
When Peter saw him, he asked, "Lord, what about him?" Jesus answered, "If I want him to remain alive until I return, what is that to you? You must follow me." Because of this, the rumor spread among the believers that this disciple would not die. But Jesus did not say that he would not die; he only said, "If I want him to remain alive until I return, what is that to you?"

God is saying there is a danger in distractions.

In this passage of scripture, we hear Jesus asking the disciple Peter a question, "Loveth thou me more than these?"

Peter replied, "Yes, Lord."

"Feed my sheep."

In the midst of Jesus giving him instructions on the call on his life, Peter asked about John's future and call. Jesus rebuked Peter and in so many words told him, "Don't worry about what I'm doing or going to do in John's future; you need to concentrate on what I told you to do."

It is my belief we miss out and find ourselves out of God's will for our life because we're so busy listening and looking at someone else's future and what they're doing. We need to hear God's instruction for our future, meditate on it, consecrate it and do it. Distraction can mean destruction.

# Prayerful Reflection

# Prayerful Reflection

# Bubble Bath or Pure Water

**SCRIPTURE: 1 Peter 2:1-3**
Therefore, rid yourselves of all malice and all deceit, hypocrisy, envy, and slander of every kind. Like newborn babies, crave pure spiritual milk, so that by it you may grow up in your salvation, now that you have tasted that the Lord is good.

One day as I got up to do my routine of taking a bath, I noticed I had run out of bubble bath. Once I finished bathing, I had a dirt ring around the bathtub and some dirt on the surface of the tub. I was really surprised and indignant how the "bubble bath" hid how dirty I really was. The Holy Spirit revealed to me at that moment, "Bubble bath" hid my dirt and had me thinking I was cleaner than I actually was. How the Word of God will reveal to one how dirty one really is, but one can sometimes substitute God's Word with **gospel** music, tapes of inspirational speakers, preachers, prophets, listening to gospel radio stations, watching televangelists and peering into one's pastor's eyes as he preaches the Word and they proclaim how many blessings one is going to receive in spite of how one may be living, and taking every word one hears as truth. Without reading, studying and applying God's word to one's life, one is getting a "bubble bath". The Word of God says, "Crave pure spiritual milk, so that by it, you may grow up in your salvation, now that you have tasted that the Lord Is good."

Ladies, it's time to grow up. Just as the "bubble bath" deceived me to believe I was cleaner than I really was, I didn't realize how dirty I actually was until I ran out of it. Are you being deceived? The enemy wants those of us who have a personal relationship with God to think since we've been saved and committed, at church all week, not fornicating etcetera; that we have arrived. However, that morning, it was revealed to me that I wasn't as clean as I thought I was and there is much room for growth, maturing and cleansing from sin. For those who have not received Christ as one's personal Saviour, know that listening to gospel music and having "Never Would have Made It" for one's ringtone still leaves you without a Savior and salvation, and the bubble bath one is getting is covering up the dirt in one's life, which is sin. See, by me having a personal relationship with God, I recognized the coverup, because the Holy Spirit revealed it and I received the message and rebuke; however, without relationship, there is no revelation.

# Prayerful Reflection

# Prayerful Reflection

# Possess It or Lose it

Deuteronomy 1:5-8 & Romans 12: 1-2

To make sure that we are in God's perfect will, evidenced through the Word of God. God says to present your bodies as a living sacrifice, holy and pleasing to God, which is your reasonable service. Then we can prove what is good and acceptable and perfect will of God; therefore, being in position for possession of the promise.

We must realize when we're not in God's perfect will, we stand to lose out on the promise even though we don't lose our position in the Kingdom of God.

Just as Moses, due to disobedience, saw the promised land but did not enter in to possess it; he lost the possession but did not lose position in the Kingdom of God. Some are satisfied with just getting into Heaven. However, the women of Unfolding want what God has for us to possess on this side of Heaven, as well as what's on the other side of Heaven. What about you?"

# Prayerful Reflection

# Changing Familiar Approaches and Practices

ST JOHN 21: 1-5

God wants to enlarge our borders. Be what he wants us to be and show us the other side and take us from the familiar so that we can obtain greater revelation, vision purpose and ultimately destiny. The disciples fished all night in familiar water and caught nothing 1. God didn't change their gift and talent for fishing, but he changed their approach. Jesus called to them, "Friends! Haven't you caught any fish?"

"No," they answered.

Jesus instructed them not to come out of the boat or stop fishing. He instructed them to specifically change direction and put the net on the right side of the boat. Hearing Jesus, no one questioned His direction; they obeyed His voice. In obedience, they came up with abundance and were unable to haul the net in because of the large number of fish.

God wants to do the same thing in our life. But, we have to be willing to change familiar approaches so God can enlarge our boundaries!

For those of you who have been with this Ministry for the past 10 plus years for our retreats and other programs, you know us, "**We Keep** It **Real.**" If you are tired of casting your net in familiar areas of your life and coming up with nothing, maybe God is trying to take you in another direction or trying to lead you into a different approach and/or territory. Cast your net to the other side and trust in GOD to lead you to destiny.

# Prayerful Reflection

# Prayerful Reflection

# The Prerequisites for Restoration Repentance, Forgiveness and Acceptance
Luke 15:11-31

The word restoration was in my spirit months before this was penned; however, immediately, I thought about the area in my life that I felt I was having the greatest struggle in, and that would be where God would start restoring, which was my finances. If that was done, I would have been able to get some of the things I **wanted and pay** some things off **etcetera**. However, God stopped me in my tracks! He said, "**There are some Prerequisites** for **Restoration.**" God showed me in the above scripture that restoration must start with reconciliation to Him; and in order to be reconciled to Him; there must be a sincere process of repentance, forgiveness and acceptance.

Just as the "Prodigal **Son**" while in his pig pen experience had to first acknowledge he had sinned by doing his own thing and leaving the father behind, we, too, must repent and return to the Father first. His father immediately began the restoration process; seeing his child far off with a true repentant heart. He had compassion, ran to the son and gave him a kiss. God then revealed to me that there are still some areas in the prerequisites I needed to deal with before my restoration process could begin. For example, if I wanted my finances restored, I needed to first repent for how I had mismanaged them, had not been a good steward, and acknowledge I **was** doing my own thing at times. Then I had to accept the part I played in my pig pen experience as it relates to my finances, accept the Father's forgiveness, forgive others, and accept what the Father wants to give me.

The first thing the **"Prodigal Son"** said was, "I'm not worthy to be called son." Only God can determine my worth. As it relates to the brother, I cannot be jealous and bitter about what God wants to bless others with, whom I feel the pig pen experience was worse than mine.

In our Christian walk; all of us can benefit from true repentance, true forgiveness and true acceptance in some area of our life.

# Prayerful Reflection

# Prayerful Reflection

# Scarred for Life

**Scripture: Isaiah 59:5**

I broke out with bumps all over my body from head to toe. I went to the doctor and one of my main concerns was: will the bumps leave scars?'

The doctor answered that no, they would go away.

While in thought, the Holy Spirit spoke to me and reminded me that Jesus still bore the scars from calvary, which is a reminder of his Love For me: I was so concerned about the outward appearance of my scars and what people may think or say, I forgot about the message behind the scars. **Isaiah 53:5 tells us: "But He was pierced for our transgressions, He was crushed for our iniquities, the punishment that brought us peace was upon** Him, **and by** His **wounds we are healed."** Jesus never gave it a thought about what people would think; He was looking at the victory behind the scars.

Therefore, we have scars, too, so we can remember the pain we may have gone through, but—more importantly—through our pain, came our healing. Jesus had to go through much pain and suffering for us to gain the victory of the cross. We may have been scarred inwardly or outwardly, or both these are scars that can bring us victory on this side of Heaven. That's why God said, "Scarred for Life," because we can look at our scars and they can be a reminder of where we have been, where we are, and where we want to go. Jesus knew His scars were taking Him somewhere; and those scars would be used for ultimate victory over death and the Glory of God the Father. Now that I have been healed from those terrible bumps that itched and got worse at night to where I couldn't sleep, when the doctor told me that I must have hugged someone, touched someone with scabies, it made me very cautious now with whom I'm touching and what I'm touching and whom I'm hugging, because I don't want to experience those (bumps) scars again.

Our scars and wounds are designed as reminders of good or bad, but we choose if we're going to use them for victory for ourselves and for others. Your scars and wounds are taking you somewhere victorious if you will choose the path God has for you. Please be cautious; please watch whom you're touching and what the message is you're giving and to whom you're giving it. Yes, your scars and wounds have a story behind them, but they're designed to bring life, not death, just as our Savior's scars and wounds brought us eternal life.

# Prayerful Reflection

# Kept for Purpose
Psalms 30

One day while sitting at work just doing my job, I was suddenly overcome by the Holy Spirit, the spirit of praise that I could not ignore and I chose not to quench. I was just thanking the Lord. In that hour, I began to look back over my life and think about all of the things God didn't allow me to go through.

Even though I used drugs, I didn't become an addict; I didn't lose control, or lose my children, go into rehab, sell my body, or even obtain a felony record. I was not molested, and even when someone tried, God intervened and didn't allow that to happen. So much more went through my mind, but what I kept asking God through my praise was why did you keep me? Then God placed me over a ministry to help those who have experienced what He didn't allow in my life. What an awesome God we serve! Truly, His ways are not our ways, neither His thoughts are our thoughts. This is not at all to suggest that those who went through some or all of these things are any better or worse than I am. God allowed this observation for purpose. Keep reading.

I left work, and the praise continued in my car; I could not stop praising and thanking God and crying. However, while pumping my gas and sitting in the car, the Holy Spirit said in a still, small voice, "You were kept for purpose." I could only praise God even more.

In spite of all the traps and snares that the enemy has set for us, God has allowed you and me to be "Kept for Purpose". What has God allowed you to be kept for?

Maybe God allowed you to meet some fates I didn't, but nevertheless, we have all been "Kept for Purpose". Are you dwelling on your misfortunes? Are you thinking I didn't go through that, or I didn't do drugs, or maybe someone deserved what happened to them? Any of those thoughts would be wrong. Whatever you have gone through, there is a purpose for it, and God wants to use everything we have gone through for His glory and for our edification. What purpose has God kept you for?

# Prayerful Reflection

# Prayerful Reflection

# Fulfilled Deficiency

Acts 18 23-28

Apollos was a learned man with a thorough knowledge of the scripture. However, he knew only of the baptism of John the Baptist. Therefore, he was deficient in having the full knowledge of God, until Priscilla and Aquilla explained God's way more adequately. Perhaps, you may need to know more about our Lord and Savior Jesus Christ and what He required of you in order to fix the deficiency in your life.

I'm sure we all have had a unique experience with meeting our Lord and Savior Jesus Christ. However, just *as* Apollos, one may still be in deficit. Until he was taught and educated, he thought he had all he needed to know. Moreover, due to the sincerity of his heart, God brought him into total truth.

You may be one who's saying to themselves, I've been doing what I feel God wants me to do. But, somehow I feel deficient. Have you totally allowed God to be Lord in every area of your life? Are you teachable? Or do you know it all?

# Prayerful Reflection

# Cut Off, Pruned or Die

John 15: 1-7

One day while cleaning my office at work, I looked on my file cabinet where I had a plant, and I also had one on the window sill. I had neglected these plants, which were both gifts to me, for so long that they were dying. So, I watered the plants, and at that moment, the Holy Spirit spoke to me and said, "Due to you neglecting the plants for so long, they will need more than watering; if you don't cut off the dead leaves, you will infect the rest of the plant and the whole plant will eventually die, and if it's dead, throw it away."

I know today that the plants needed more than just watering. I had to throw away the old soil (sin), and give plant food, (the Word of God), cut off the dead branches, (people, places, and things), watering the plants, (being filled with the Holy Spirit), while making sure they get plenty of light, (Jesus Christ), and I have to do this on a regular basis. If I'm not willing to do all of the above, the gifts will die. In the commentary dealing with our scripture of reference, John 15:1-7, it stated Christ could have been referring to a physical death of a fruitless Christian, or hoping we would respond and begin to bear fruit and live, as noted in that 6th verse.

We need to allow God to use the gifts He's given us, and give Him permission to throw away the parts that have attached themselves to us and are choking us, leaving us fruitless. We must allow God to do the pruning in our life so we can bear even more fruit for His glory. We need to allow the Holy Spirit to abide in us so the gift that is in us will flourish. Don't just water down your gift; nurture, prune, cherish and use the gift in you.

# Prayerful Reflection

# Prayerful Reflection

# A PARTIAL CONNECTION

Ezekiel 37: 1-5

On Christmas morning, I was talking to my son, who did a three-way and called his sister. I walked into the kitchen while talking with them and began to prepare myself some breakfast. In the midst of this, we got off the phone and when hanging up, I said, "I meant to tell them about my dream." I called my daughter back and began to share with her how I had meant to share my dream with her and her brother. Just I began to speak, my cell phone died. I said, "No way my phone died that quick, I had it plugged in all-night." As I walked back to my bedroom and saw the cord on my bed, I said, "I knew I had my phone plugged in." When I walked over to the other side of my bed, I looked down on the floor and saw the other end of the cord was not plugged into the electricity, so the end I saw on the bed was plugged into the phone all night but the other end was not connected to the power source. The Holy Spirit immediately gave me the theme "A Partial Connection."

It is much more dangerous to think you have power and have very little than to know you have no power at all. Do not let the enemy deceive you, whether we are connected to God or not. There is no such thing as "A Partial Connection". I was really walking around with a dead phone (Dead Bones). It was just a matter of time for it to be revealed. Some of us are dead bones walking around and it just has not been revealed; the partial connection is no connection at all and renders us powerless when life shows up. That phone was not connected to the power source, but I was led to believe I had power, but really, I had enough power to deceive me that I had a connection to the source.

The above brings me to what else the Lord spoke to me in that moment, how a partial connection only gives deception of power that is not lasting and can prove dangerous in the perilous times in which we are living in this very season. We must be sure we are completely connected to God, anything less than that is "A Partial Connection". I asked God what scripture He wanted me to use for this theme He had given me? What immediately dropped in my spirit was Ezekiel 37: "Can these dry bones live?" The Prophet Ezekiel was led to see the dead bones in the land, and I have seen the devastation (dead bones) in our land, death all around us, but most of all, the spiritual deadness in the world and in the body of Christ. Drugs, killings, child abuse, sickness, sexual lust, disease, mental illness (perilous times), you name it. I have been asked the question can these dead bones live, and as Ezekiel turned the question back to God, so did I. Yes, with God, all things are possible, but in order to change the dead things in our life as well as helping this spiritually dying world's total connection to the power, it is found only in total surrender to the power source, which is our Lord and Savior Jesus Christ. Are you connected? Alternatively, do we have "A Partial Connection"?

# Prayerful Reflection

# KEEP PLUGGED IN; SO WE WON'T CONTINUE TO LOSE OUR VALUABLE JEWELS

**PSALMS 27:14** "WAIT patiently FOR THE LORD BE BRAVE AND COURAGEOUS. YES WAIT PATIENTLY FOR THE LORD" **(NIV)**

One day while brushing my teeth, I took the plug out of the sink. The reason I took the plug out is because the water will run out faster. I'm impatient and don't want to wait; however, by doing this, I have lost several valuable jewels, necklaces, and random earrings, even though I know this has happened over and over and I still believe I'm fast enough or careful enough to catch my valuables before they go down the drain. While in mid-thought of this, the Holy Spirit spoke to my heart about my unwillingness to wait and to allow the plug to do what it is designed to do.

What is the Holy Spirit speaking to you about being inpatient and not waiting on God? Where are you today in using the tools God has provided you with to save your valuable Jewels? Are you running out on your true blessing?

While continuing to pray about what God had given to me, an employee brought something that he had downloaded on his phone into my office. He stated, "I do not know why I had to show this to you but when I read it, I thought about you."

When I began to read this, it blew me **away**. It only confirmed what our God is saying to each of us. Please hear what our God is speaking to us, and it reads as follows: Queens, you are more precious than diamonds, pearls and gold! You are fearfully and wonderfully made.

Wonderful are God's works; your soul knows Him very well. Two young women arrived at a meeting wearing clothes that were quite revealing of their body parts.

Here is what the chairman told them. He took a good look at them and made them sit down. Then he **said** something that they might never forget in their life. He looked them straight in the eyes and said, "Ladies, everything that God made valuable in this world is well-covered and protected and hard to see, find or get."

1.      Where do you find diamonds? Deep down in the ground, covered and protected.
2.      Where do you find pearls? Deep down at the bottom of the ocean, covered up and protected in a beautiful shell.
3.      Where do you find gold? Way down in the mine, covered over with layers of rock, and to get them, you have to work hard and dig deep down.

He looked at them with serious eyes and said, "Your body is sacred and unique; you are far more precious than gold, diamonds and pearls, and you should be covered too."

# Prayerful Reflection

# ONE WAY TO BE HEALED; TAKE THE PAIN

Isaiah 53:3-4

I hit my toe on a wrought iron chair in my upstairs hallway. It was so painful, and even though I had hit it before, never to this degree. It brought tears to my eyes. I said, "Lord Jesus, that hurt so bad." The question came to me, "Why won't you move the chair?" Sometimes it takes this level of pain to get our attention, because we will not move, remove, or get rid of the thing, or things, in our life that are causing pain without a very painful experience.

Through this process, I learned several valuable lessons. If I had moved the chair the first time I hit my toe, I wouldn't have hit it a second, third, or possibly a fourth time. When God provides an escape, or tells you to move or remove something or someone, we need to do it immediately. I thought it was just bruised, but with so much pain, I was led to go to the physical doctor, who could give me the truth. The doctor said it was broken and he could tape it together and put me in a soft shoe, give me muscle relaxers and pain medication, but he also said, "It will have to heal itself and it will be painful." Therefore, what the doctor said to me is, "You're going to have to go through the pain to get to the healing. That was in the physical, but there is another doctor, the master physician, Jesus Christ, who is the healing process for his children. "For he was wounded for our transgressions, he was bruised for our iniquities; the chastisement of our peace was upon him; and with his stripes we are healed." No Christian is exempt from going through some pain, whether we caused it, someone else caused it, or God allowed it. But thanks be unto God, because of the cross, whatever type of pain we are in, we can be healed. Will you be healed today? Are you willing to go through the pain for your healing?

Are you broken? Are you bruised? Are you fractured? Whichever place you're in, the healing process is the same. You may be heartbroken, you may have lost a loved one, you may be in a relationship that has left you bruised; wherever you are in your life, broken, bruised or fractured, there is only one anecdote for your healing. Come out and hear a few women teach and speak about "one way to be healed, take the pain:" how they walked through their pain and how they received their healing.

# Prayerful Reflection

# Prayerful Reflection

# TIIE MISFIT
## 1 Corinthians 1:27-29

To inform some and remind others that salvation is extended to all mankind. Regardless of one's status in life, Jesus died for you. You are a usable vessel. Unfolding Truth Ministry is back once again with a powerful revelation from the Holy Spirit. Have you been downtrodden, looked down upon, and made to feel that you would never amount to anything? Just a total "MISFIT".

There have been other women who may have had the above feelings. However, God said, "Not so!" God has instructed six women to tell you that you fit right into His program.

God used the following individuals to assure us today that the DEVIL IS A LIAR!

| | | |
|---|---|---|
| MARY MAGDALENE | M- | MISSION |
| ESTHER | I - | INSTRUMENT |
| SAMARITAN WOMAN | S- | SAVED |
| RAHAB | F- | FAITH |
| HANNAH | I- | INTIMATE |
| GOMER | T - | TRANSFORMED |

# Prayerful Reflection

# Prayerful Reflection

# 70 years God Bore Noah's Embarrassment

Hebrews 11:1-7

One day while sitting at my desk again, I looked on my computer monitor and taped to it were these words, "70 YEARS, GOD BORE NOAH'S EMBARRASSMENT." When I read those words, I said, "I don't remember when I wrote that or where it came from, but, Lord, is this the theme for our next event?" No answer at that moment. I shared it with my best friend and she said, "Wow." We both said we are going to keep praying and see what God is saying.

Well, Saturday of that same week, August 13, 2016, the Holy Spirit spoke to my heart as I walked through my house, cleaning. He said, "He has borne my embarrassments, ridicule, shame and fears the same way He did for Noah." God made a promise to Noah but gave specific instruction on what he needed to do, to bring this prophecy to pass. Noah said, "It's going to rain." He was laughed at, taunted, and called a fool, I'm sure. I can relate to Noah's dilemma; I, too, have experienced all of the above. But Noah kept walking, hearing and obeying God, and when the flood came, Noah received the promise of him and his family being spared. Sometimes the payoff may seem trivial at the time; it took "70" years for it to rain and eight lives spared, and Noah had to go through all he did for just that. But a whole world was born from eight people and two of each of God's animal kingdom. I have thought that as well at times about this Ministry, "25" YEARS. Must I continue to go through so much so that God can get the glory for such a small return? But I can truly say that my faith has caught up with my belief, my walking, my talking and my waiting, and the payoff has been too great to pen. Know today that God has borne our shame, our embarrassment, the laughs and fears.

Whatever He told you, He is able to bring it to pass, but your faith has to catch up with your belief. It took more than belief from Noah; it took faith. It was once said to me, "A faith that can't be tested is a faith that can't be trusted."

# Prayerful Reflection

# Prayerful Reflection

_____
_____
_____
_____
_____
_____
_____
_____
_____
_____
_____
_____
_____
_____
_____
_____
_____
_____
_____

# *POSSESS IT OR LOSE IT*

HOW DO WE POSSESS OUR PROMISE? HOW DO WE LOSE OUR WILL?

HOW DO WE LEARN TO TRUST GOD'S DIRECTION, NOT BASED ON HOW WE FEEL?

HOW DO WE MOVE FROM DEPRESSION?

HOW DO WE LET GO AND LET GOD?

BY LISTENING AND OBEYING AGAINST ALL ODDS, HOW DO WE LOSE OUR PROMISE?

BY NOT HEARING AND OBEYING AND PUTTING LIMITS ON GOD BY NOT TAKING A STAND, BECAUSE WE FEAR MAN MORE THAN GOD.

BY NOT LAUNCHING INTO THE DEEP, THEREFORE, ALLOWING FEAR TO BE OUR DEFEAT.

THEREFORE, I REPEAT, "POSSESS IT OR LOSE IT." OR LIVE IN DEFEAT.

*INSPIRED BY GOD!*

*WRITTEN BY: EVANGELIST SHELIA GRIGGS-PARKER*

# "THE BEAUTY OF A ROSE"

*When she was a child,* she saw the beauty in a rose. When she pricked her finger, she threw the rose down, and no longer does *the rose leave a* smile, but a frown.

When one is hurt as a child by rejection or abuse, one may feel what's the use?

When one is hurt as a child, they may bury the truth, therefore, it can grow into a bitter root. When one harbors these hurts and we won't forgive, we don't see our rose petals, it's *the pricks we feel.* The pricks one may have received as a child God can use/or his glory to turn someone's frown into a smile.

*I tell you the truth, the one who made the rose also made you. When God created the rose, he put pricks there so one would have to handle it delicately and with care.*

*When He made women, he made us with the same thought in mind, to be handled like a rose, loved tenderly and treated kindly.*

*When you look at this picture, concentrate on "THE BEAUTY OF A ROSE" as a whole and include yourself in that equation and remember that God made the pricks as well as the rose.*

# **WHAT DO YOU DO?**

WHAT DO YOU DO WHEN YOU FEEL ALL ALONE?
WHAT DO YOU DO WHEN YOU FEEL ALL HOPE IS GONE?
WHAT DO YOU DO WHEN YOU FEEL LIFELESS?
WHAT DO YOU DO WHEN YOU FEEL JUST HELPLESS?
WHAT DO YOU DO WHEN THE WORLD FEELS LIKE IT IS CLOSING IN ON YOU?
WHAT DO YOU DO WHEN FRIENDS TURN THEIR BACK ON YOU TOO?
WHAT DO YOU DO WHEN YOU'RE LIED ABOUT?
WHAT DO YOU DO WHEN NO ONE BELIEVES YOU AT ALL?
WHAT DO YOU DO WHEN YOUR DREAMS TURN INTO DISAPPOINTMENTS?
WHAT DO YOU DO WHEN YOU FEEL LIFE IS FALLING DOWN ALL AROUND YOU?

WHAT DO YOU DO WHEN YOU WANT YOUR LIFE TO END?

WHAT DO YOU DO WHEN FEAR GRIPS YOUR SOUL BUT YOU KNOW YOU'VE BEEN BORN AGAIN?

YOU CRY OUT TO GOD WITH MOANS AND GROANS THAT ONLY THE HOLY SPIRIT CAN SPEAK.

YOU KEEP RUNNING TO THE ARMS OF JESUS, REACHING TO TOUCH THE END OF HIS GARMENT AND EVEN HIS FEET.

YOU KEEP REACHING FOR HIS PRESENCE THROUGH SINGING, PRAYING WHILE WAITING FOR ANSWERS.

YOU KEEP SEEKING TO HEAR HIM. THROUGH HIS WORD HIS VOICE WILL SPEAK.

YOU STAND ON WHAT YOU KNOW IN YOUR HEART ABOUT THE DEVIL'S DEFEAT.

YOU REMEMBER PASS VICTORY, WHICH WILL LIFT YOUR SPIRIT TO PRAISE.

YOU THANK GOD IN THE MIDST OF THE STORM AND GLORIFY HIS NAME.

YOU WILL FEEL YOUR SPIRIT LIFTING AND A PRAISE IN YOUR HEART.

YOU WILL GET RENEWED STRENGTH TO KEEP MOVING FORWARD IN SPITE OF YOUR TRIALS.

YOU STAND ON THE FOUNDATION THAT GOD HAS GIVEN YOU THROUGH HIS ONLY BEGOTTEN SON WHO DIED ON THE CROSS FOR YOU.

YOU GIVE GOD THE GLORY FOR HEARING YOUR HUMBLE CRY AND FOR WIPING THE TEARS FROM YOUR WEEPING EYES.

YOU WILL FEEL THE BURDEN LIFTING AND YOUR FEET FILLED WITH PRAISE.

WHEN I THINK OF GOD'S GOODNESS AND ALL HE'S DONE FOR ME, MY SOUL CRIES OUT HALLELUJAH. THANK YOU FOR RELIEVING ME.

# Prayerful Reflection

# About the Author

Minister, Shelia Denise Griggs-Parker is an ordained Evangelist and Minister of the Gospel. She has been commissioned, ordained and sent by God to go to the high places, the low places and the valley's and speak God's Word. If asked who sent me? Tell them I AM sent me. I am a teacher, motivational speaker, preacher and advocate for the truth of God's Word.

I'm a Licensed Independent Chemical Dependency Counselor, I received my MSSA from Case Western Reserve University. I have a passion and a call to help provide individuals with hope, challenging them to affirm themselves through the lens of God; but, allowing them to choose their own affirming belief. My church home is True Vine House of Deliverance, where my Pastor/Husband proceeded me in death.

To connect with Minister Parker, send an email to divanmotion.pod@gmail.com, ministergriggsparker@gmail.com or sheliagriggs56@gmail.com.

www.ingramcontent.com/pod-product-compliance
Lightning Source LLC
Chambersburg PA
CBHW072200160426
43197CB00012B/2461